CLIP ART FOR THE LITURGICAL YEAR

CLIP ART

FOR THE LITURGICAL YEAR

Designs by
CLEMENS SCHMIDT

Edited by
JOSHUA J. JEIDE, O.S.B.

THE LITURGICAL PRESS
Collegeville, Minnesota 56321

Copyright © 1988 by The Order of St. Benedict, Inc.
All rights reserved.

The art in this book may be reproduced in bulletins, programs, and announcements prepared by non-commercial organizations such as parishes and schools. The art may not be reproduced for commercial use without written permission of the copyright holder.

Printed in the United States of America.
ISBN 0-8146-1582-1

CONTENTS

DEDICATION

This volume is dedicated to the memory of Clemens Schmidt (1901–1984), a distinguished liturgical artist whose work has been published extensively by The Liturgical Press. The designs are printed here in black for use as clip art. In Schmidt's originals this work appeared in two colors or in full color.

A native of Wiesbaden, West Germany, and a student of Professor Rudolf Koch, Schmidt spent ten years as a graphic artist with Mathias Grünewald Publications, Mainz and Wiesbaden, before establishing his own studio at age thirty-seven.

Schmidt's artistry has been expressed in stained glass, vestments, metal and silver work, ceramics, stone, graphic design, and calligraphy. He was keenly interested in the arts of the Church and in themes concerning the Bible and liturgy. For over thirty years his designs and calligraphy appeared in publications of The Liturgical Press, particularly in the *Bible and Liturgy Sunday Bulletins*. Other examples of his work are found in churches in West Germany and in three churches in Ohio.

PRE
PARE
THE
WAY
FOR
THE
LORD,
SMOOTHEN
THE PATH
FOR OUR GOD

1a.

RORATE COELI DESUPER

ET NUBES PLUANT JUSTUM

PRE
PARE
THE
WAY
FOR
THE
LORD,
SMOOTHEN
THE PATH
FOR OUR GOD

1b.

RORATE COELI DESUPER

ET NUBES PLUANT JUSTUM

RORATE COELI DESUPER

ET NUBES PLUANT JUSTUM

make
READY
the
way
of the
LORD

1d.

make
READY
the
way
of the
LORD

1c.

BEDEW US, HEAVEN FROM
ABOVE, YE CLOUDS
RAIN DOWN THE JUST ONE

BEDEW US, HEAVEN FROM
ABOVE, YE CLOUDS
RAIN DOWN THE JUST ONE

3a.

3b.

GAUDETE

3c.

5a.

NOW THE LORD IS NIGH COME LET US APORE

5b. NOW THE LORD IS NIGH COME LET US APORE

NOW THE LORD IS NIGH COME LET US APORE

NOW THE LORD IS NIGH COME LET US APORE

NOW THE LORD IS NIGH COME LET US APORE

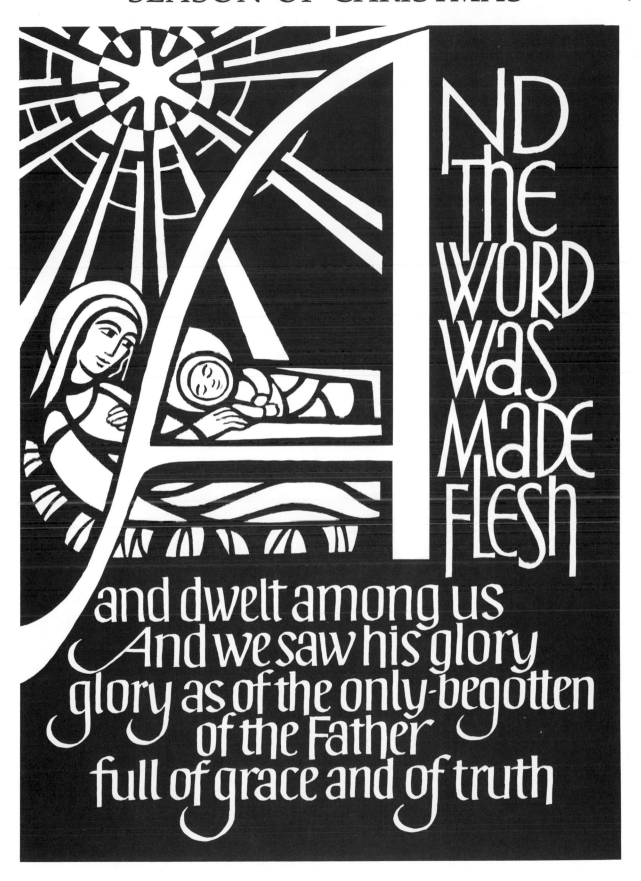

And the word was made flesh and dwelt among us And we saw his glory glory as of the only-begotten of the Father full of grace and of truth

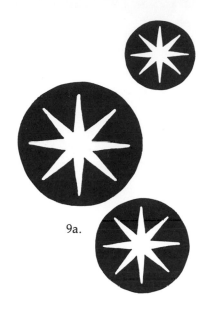

9a.

9b.

Because the maker of us all lay with the cattle in the stall

Because the great comes to the small I thank my God

Because the maker of us all lay with the cattle in the stall

Because the great comes to the small I thank my God

9c.

Because the maker of us all lay with the cattle in the stall

Because the great comes to the small I thank my God

11a.

A GRAND MYSTERY!
A WONDROUS SACRAMENT!
ANIMALS LOOK AT THE NEWBORN LORD
LYING IN THE CRIB.
BLESSED ARE YOU, O VIRGIN,
FOR YOUR WOMB WAS PRIVILEGED
TO BEAR CHRIST THE LORD!

11b.

A GRAND MYSTERY!
A WONDROUS SACRAMENT!
ANIMALS LOOK AT THE NEWBORN LORD
LYING IN THE CRIB.
BLESSED ARE YOU, O VIRGIN,
FOR YOUR WOMB WAS PRIVILEGED
TO BEAR CHRIST THE LORD!

SING TO THE LORD
A NEW CANTICLE ALLELUJA
FOR THE LORD HAS DONE
WONDROUS DEEDS+

13a.

SING TO THE LORD
A NEW CANTICLE ALLELUJA
FOR THE LORD HAS DONE
WONDROUS DEEDS+

Behold, the Name
of the Lord
comes from afar,
and His glory fills
the whole world

13b.

Behold, the Name
of the Lord
comes from afar,
and His glory fills
the whole world

Behold, the Name
of the Lord
comes from afar,
and His glory fills
the whole world

SEASON OF CHRISTMAS

15a.

15b.

15c.

15d.

YOU HAVE APPEARED, O CHRIST, THE LIGHT OF LIGHT! TO YOU THE MAGI BRING GIFTS! ALLELUJA · ALLELUJA!

19a.

YOU HAVE APPEARED, O CHRIST, THE LIGHT OF LIGHT! TO YOU THE MAGI BRING GIFTS! ALLELUJA · ALLELUJA!

19b.

21a.

21b.

21c.

23a.

Behold/this Child
is destined for the fall
and for the rise of
many in Israel/and for
a sign that shall
be contradicted

Behold/this Child
is destined for the fall
and for the rise of
many in Israel/and for
a sign that shall
be contradicted

23b.

23c.

25a.

25b.

25c.

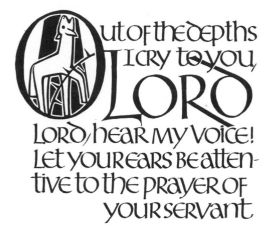

Out of the depths I cry to you, O LORD LORD, HEAR MY VOICE! LET YOUR EARS BE ATTENtive to the prayer of YOUR SERVANT

27a.

Out of the depths I cry to you, O LORD LORD, HEAR MY VOICE! LET YOUR EARS BE ATTENtive to the prayer of YOUR SERVANT

Out of the depths I cry to you, O LORD LORD, HEAR MY VOICE! LET YOUR EARS BE ATTENtive to the prayer of YOUR SERVANT

27b.

As the sufferings of christ abound in us+ so also through christ does our comfort abound

As the sufferings of christ abound in us+ so also through christ does our comfort abound

27c.

SEASON OF THE

29a.

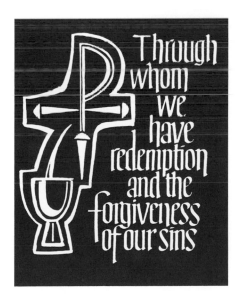

29b.

31a.

THROUGH THY CROSS AND PASSION
O LORD + DELIVER US

THROUGH THY CROSS AND PASSION
O LORD + DELIVER US

31b.

31c.

THROUGH THY CROSS AND PASSION
O LORD + DELIVER US

31d.

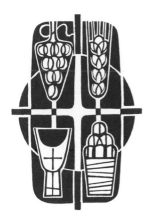

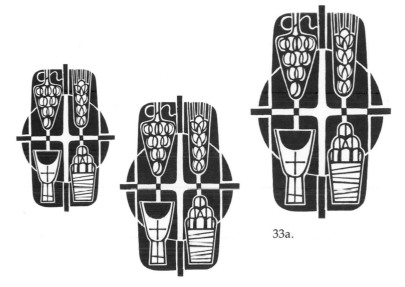

33a.

As priest Jesus offered his life on the altar of the cross and redeemed the human race by this one perfect sacrifice of praise

33b.

As priest Jesus offered his life on the altar of the cross and redeemed the human race by this one perfect sacrifice of praise

35a.

35b.

35c.

37a.

christ became
obedient
for us unto
death
even to death
on a CROSS

37b.

christ became
obedient
for us unto
death
even to death
on a CROSS

37c.

By the Cross
her vigil keeping,
Stands the mournful
Mother weeping,
Near her Son
until the end +

37d.

Look down upon me, good and gentle Jesus, while before Your face I humbly come, ✝ and with burning soul pray and beseech You to fix deep in my heart lively sentiments of faith, hope, and charity, of true contrition for my sins and a firm purpose of amendment — the while I contemplate with great love and tender pity Your five most precious wounds, pondering over them within me, and calling to mind the words which David, Your prophet, said of You, my Jesus: "They have pierced my hands and feet, they have numbered all my bones."

We adore You, O Christ, and we praise You. ✝ Because by Your holy Cross You have redeemed the world

41a.

41b.

We adore You, O Christ, and we praise You. ✝ Because by Your holy Cross You have redeemed the world

41c.

We adore You, O Christ, and we praise You. ✝ Because by Your holy Cross You have redeemed the world

**BY THY
HOLY CROSS
THOU HAST
REDEEMED THE
WORLD**

43a.

**BY THY
HOLY CROSS
THOU HAST
REDEEMED THE
WORLD**

**BY THY
HOLY CROSS
THOU HAST
REDEEMED THE
WORLD**

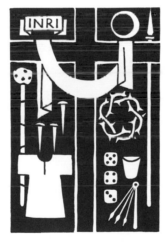

43b.

FOR BY A
SINGLE
OFFERING
HE HAS
PERFECTED
FOR ALL
TIME THOSE
WHO ARE
SANCTIFIED

FOR BY A
SINGLE
OFFERING
HE HAS
PERFECTED
FOR ALL
TIME THOSE
WHO ARE
SANCTIFIED

FOR BY A
SINGLE
OFFERING
HE HAS
PERFECTED
FOR ALL
TIME THOSE
WHO ARE
SANCTIFIED

43c.

At that time Mary Magdalene, and Mary the Mother of James, and Salome, bought perfumed oils, intending to come and anoint Jesus. Then, very early in the morning, on the first day of the week, they came to the tomb, after sunrise. They were saying to one another, Who will roll back the stone for us from the entrance to the tomb? But when they looked up, they observed that the stone had been rolled back, and it was indeed huge. On entering the tomb, they saw a young man sitting at the right, dressed in a white robe. This thoroughly amazed them. But he reassured them, No need to be amazed! You are looking for Jesus of Nazareth, the crucified. He has been raised: he is not here. See the spot where they laid him. Now go, tell his disciples and Peter, he is going to Galilee ahead of you, where you will see him, just as He told you

ALLELUIA

47a.

But the angel
spoke and said
to the women
Do not be
afraid, for I
know that
you seek
Jesus, who
was crucified +
he is not here, for he has
risen even as he said
Alleluja·Alleluja Alleluja

47b.

But the angel
spoke and said
to the women
Do not be
afraid, for I
know that
you seek
Jesus, who
was crucified +
he is not here, for he has
risen even as he said
Alleluja·Alleluja Alleluja

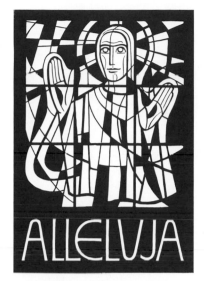

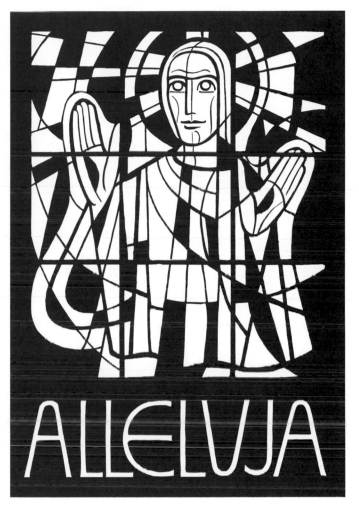

49a.

49b.

FOR THE
SPLENDORS
OF LIFE
WE THANK THEE LORD

FOR THY
RISING IN
SPLENDOR
WE PRAISE THEE

51a.

FOR THE
SPLENDORS
OF LIFE
WE THANK THEE LORD

FOR THY
RISING IN
SPLENDOR
WE PRAISE THEE

FOR THE
SPLENDORS
OF LIFE
WE THANK THEE LORD

FOR THY
RISING IN
SPLENDOR
WE PRAISE THEE

51b.

ALLELUJA

ALLELUJA

51c.

ALLELUJA

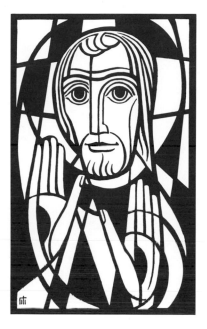

53a.

PEACE
BE TO YOU

After eight days,
the doors being closed,
Jesus came and said

PEACE
BE TO YOU
Alleluia·Alleluia

53b.

After eight days,
the doors being closed,
Jesus came and said

PEACE
BE TO YOU
Alleluia·Alleluia

PEACE
BE TO YOU

55a.

Alleluia! Christ, having risen from the dead, dies now no more + death shall no longer have dominion over him

MY LORD AND MY GOD!

55c.

55b.

Alleluia! Christ, having risen from the dead, dies now no more + death shall no longer have dominion over him

Alleluia! Christ, having risen from the dead, dies now no more + death shall no longer have dominion over him

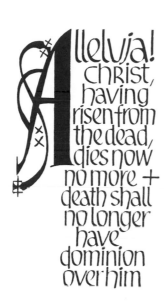

MY LORD AND MY GOD!

57a.

57b.

57c.

THE LORD, AMID TRUMPET BLASTS, ALLELUJA

59a.

THE LORD, AMID TRUMPET BLASTS, ALLELUJA

GOD ASCENDS AMID SHOUTS OF JOY, ALLELUJA

59b.

THE LORD, AMID TRUMPET BLASTS, ALLELUJA

GOD ASCENDS AMID SHOUTS OF JOY, ALLELUJA

61a.

61b.

61c.

holy Spirit, come and shine
On our souls with beams divine
Issuing from your radiance bright.
Come, O Father of the poor,
Ever bounteous of your store,
Come, our heart's unfailing light.

65b.

65a.

holy Spirit, come and shine
On our souls with beams divine
Issuing from your radiance bright.
Come, O father of the poor,
Ever bounteous of your store,
Come, our heart's unfailing light.

holy Spirit, come and shine
On our souls with beams divine
Issuing from your radiance bright.
Come, O father of the poor,
Ever bounteous of your store,
Come, our heart's unfailing light.

65c.

67a.

67b.

69b.

you
have
given us
bread
from heaven,
o Lord,
all delicate
and
sweet to
taste

you
have
given us
bread
from heaven,
o Lord,
all delicate
and
sweet to
taste

69a.

you
have
given us
bread
from heaven,
o Lord,
all delicate
and
sweet to
taste

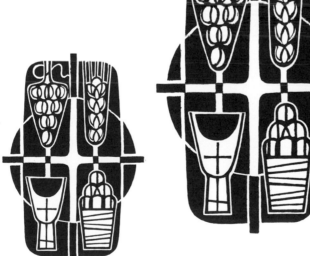

69c.

71a.

71b.

73a.

73b.

73c.

73d.

75a.

75b.

75c.

77a.

77b.

77c.

79a.

79b.

81a.

81b.

It behooved Christ to suffer these things, and so to enter into his glory

83a.

It behooved Christ to suffer these things, and so to enter into his glory

HEAVEN AND EARTH WILL PASS AWAY   BUT MY WORDS WILL NOT PASS AWAY

83b.

HEAVEN AND EARTH WILL PASS AWAY   BUT MY WORDS WILL NOT PASS AWAY

83c.

85a.

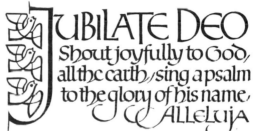

85b.

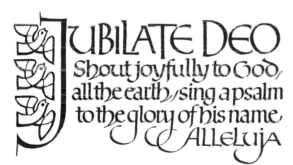

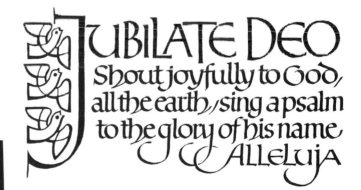

85c.

87a.

87b.

87c.

89a.

89b.

MY REFUGE
AND MY FORTRESS,
MY GOD,
IN WHOM I TRUST

MY REFUGE
AND MY FORTRESS,
MY GOD,
IN WHOM I TRUST

89c.

89d.

MY REFUGE
AND MY FORTRESS,
MY GOD,
IN WHOM I TRUST

91a.

91b.

93a.

WALK, THEN, AS CHILDREN OF LIGHT, FOR THE FRUIT OF THE LIGHT IS IN GOODNESS AND JUSTICE AND TRUTH

93b.

93c.

WALK, THEN, AS CHILDREN OF LIGHT, FOR THE FRUIT OF THE LIGHT IS IN GOODNESS AND JUSTICE AND TRUTH

MEN I SAY TO YOU all things whatever you ask for in prayer, believe that you shall receive, and they shall come to you

95a.

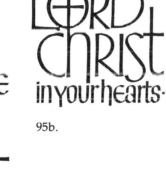

BUT hallow the LORD CHRIST in your hearts·

95b.

BUT hallow the LORD CHRIST in your hearts·

Are You the One who is to come or shall we look for another?

95c.

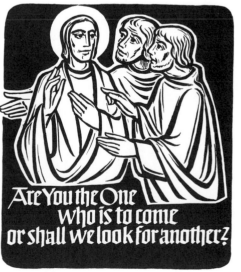

Are You the One who is to come or shall we look for another?

97a.

97b.

97c.

97d.

LORD, save us! We are perishing!

command, O GOD, and make a great calm!

99a.

99b.

LORD, save us! We are perishing!

command, O GOD, and make a great calm!

THE KINGDOM OF HEAVEN IS LIKE A NET·THAT WAS CAST INTO THE SEA AND CAUGHT FISH OF EVERY KIND· WHEN IT WAS FULL, THE FISHERMEN PULLED IT ASHORE, AND SITTING ON THE BEACH, THEY PUT THE GOOD FISH IN THEIR BUCKETS & THREW THE USELESS AWAY.

THE KINGDOM OF HEAVEN IS LIKE A NET·THAT WAS CAST INTO THE SEA AND CAUGHT FISH OF EVERY KIND· WHEN IT WAS FULL, THE FISHERMEN PULLED IT ASHORE, AND SITTING ON THE BEACH, THEY PUT THE GOOD FISH IN THEIR BUCKETS & THREW THE USELESS AWAY.

99c.

THE KINGDOM OF HEAVEN IS LIKE A NET·THAT WAS CAST INTO THE SEA AND CAUGHT FISH OF EVERY KIND· WHEN IT WAS FULL, THE FISHERMEN PULLED IT ASHORE, AND SITTING ON THE BEACH, THEY PUT THE GOOD FISH IN THEIR BUCKETS & THREW THE USELESS AWAY.

LORD *I am not worthy that Thou shouldst come under my roof*

101a.

101b.

LORD *I am not worthy that Thou shouldst come under my roof*

101c.

PEACE ✝ BE TO YOU +

PEACE ✝ BE TO YOU +

PEACE ✝ BE TO YOU +

Render, therefore
to Caesar the things
that are Caesar's,
and to God the things
that are God's

103a.

Render, therefore
to Caesar the things
that are Caesar's,
and to God the things
that are God's

Amen I say to you, unless you turn and become like little children, you will not enter the kingdom of heaven

103b.

Amen I say to you, unless you turn and become like little children, you will not enter the kingdom of heaven

GO
AND
DO THOU ALSO
IN LIKE MANNER

103c.

GO
AND
DO THOU ALSO
IN LIKE MANNER

GO
AND
DO THOU ALSO
IN LIKE MANNER

ONE LORD, FAITH, BAPTISM, GOD AND FATHER OF ALL who is above and throughout and in us

105b.

ONE LORD, FAITH, BAPTISM, GOD AND FATHER OF ALL who is above and throughout and in us

105a.

ONE LORD, FAITH, BAPTISM, GOD AND FATHER OF ALL who is above and throughout and in us

107a.

107b.

107c.

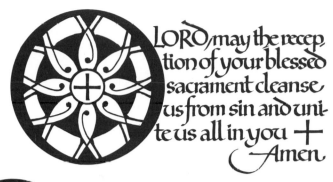

LORD, may the recep-
tion of your blessed
sacrament cleanse
us from sin and uni-
te us all in you ✝
Amen

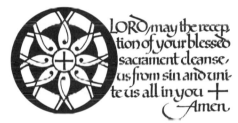

LORD, may the recep-
tion of your blessed
sacrament cleanse
us from sin and uni-
te us all in you ✝
Amen

109b.

109a.

LORD, may the recep-
tion of your blessed
sacrament cleanse
us from sin and uni-
te us all in you ✝
Amen

109c.

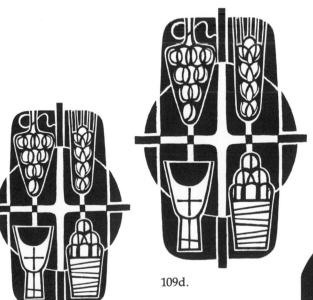

109d.

forgive
us our trespasses
+ as we
forgive
those who trespass
against us

forgive
us our trespasses
+ as we
forgive
those who trespass
against us

111a.

forgive
us our trespasses
+ as we
forgive
those who trespass
against us

111b.

THE has exercised power
RIGHT
HAND
OF THE
LORD has lifted me up +
I shall not die, but live,
and shall declare the works
of the Lord

111c.

THE has exercised power
RIGHT
HAND
OF THE
LORD has lifted me up +
I shall not die, but live,
and shall declare the works
of the Lord

113a

ALL THINGS WHATEVER YOU ASK IN PRAYER, BELIEVE THAT YOU SHALL RECEIVE AND THEY SHALL COME TO YOU

ALL THINGS WHATEVER YOU ASK IN PRAYER, BELIEVE THAT YOU SHALL RECEIVE AND THEY SHALL COME TO YOU

113b.

HE HAS DONE ALL THINGS WELL

HE HAS DONE ALL THINGS WELL

113c.

115a.

Rejoice with
those who rejoice;
weep with those
who weep.
Be of one mind
towards one
another

Rejoice with
those who rejoice;
weep with those
who weep.
Be of one mind
towards one
another

115b.

115c.

AND HE MANIFESTED HIS GLORY

115d.

AND HE MANIFESTED HIS GLORY

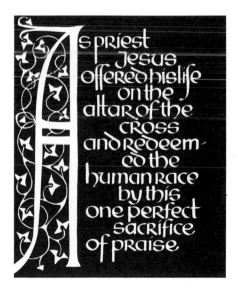

117a.

GO OUT
TO THE WHOLE
WORLD,
PROCLAIM
THE GOOD NEWS
TO ALL
CREATION

GO OUT
TO THE WHOLE
WORLD,
PROCLAIM
THE GOOD NEWS
TO ALL
CREATION

GO OUT
TO THE WHOLE
WORLD,
PROCLAIM
THE GOOD NEWS
TO ALL
CREATION

117b.

As priest
Jesus
offered his life
on the
altar of the
cross
and redeem-
ed the
human race
by this
one perfect
sacrifice
of praise

117c.

As priest
Jesus
offered his life
on the
altar of the
cross
and redeem-
ed the
human race
by this
one perfect
sacrifice
of praise

INDEX

HOLY THURSDAY

GOOD FRIDAY

EASTER SEASON

ASCENSION

PENTECOST

TRINITY SUNDAY

THE BODY AND BLOOD OF CHRIST

THE SAINTS

CHRIST THE KING

THE PSALMS

SCRIPTURE PASSAGES

Matthew	8:8	Saturday of the 12th Week in Ordinary Time	101a
		Monday of the 1st Week of Advent	101a
	8:25	Tuesday of the 13th Week in Ordinary Time	99b
	11:3	3rd Sunday of Advent (Cycle A)	95c
	13:47-48	Thursday of the 17th Week in Ordinary Time	99a
			99c
	18:3	Tuesday of the 19th Week in Ordinary Time	103b
	20:6-7	25th Sunday in Ordinary Time (Cycle A)	97b
	22:21	29th Sunday in Ordinary Time (Cycle A)	103a
	22:37-39	30th Sunday in Ordinary Time (Cycle A)	91b
Mark	11:24	Friday of the 8th Week in Ordinary Time	95a
Luke	10:37	15th Sunday in Ordinary Time (Cycle C)	103c
	11:28	Saturday of the 27th Week in Ordinary Time	93a
John	10:9	4th Sunday of Easter (Cycle A)	101b
	15:1-2	5th Sunday of Easter (Cycle B)	97c
	15:5	5th Sunday of Easter (Cycle B)	97a
	20:19	2nd Sunday of Easter (Cycle A); Pentecost	101c
Ephesians	5:8-9	4th Sunday of Lent (Cycle A)	93b
	5:20	20th Sunday in Ordinary Time (Cycle B)	91a
Colossians	3:17	Holy Family Sunday (Cycles A, B, C)	97d
1 Thessalonians	4:3	Friday of the 21st Week in Ordinary Time (Year 1)	93c
1 Peter	3:15	6th Sunday of Easter (Cycle A)	95b

SACRAMENTS OF INITIATION

BAPTISM

Baptismal symbol			105a
One Lord, one faith, one baptism	Eph 4:5-6	Calligraphy	105b

CONFIRMATION

Seven gifts of the Holy Spirit	107a
Descending dove	107b
Confirmation symbol	107c

EUCHARIST

Eucharistic symbol			109a
Lord, may the reception of your sacrament . . .		Calligraphy	109b
Loaves and fishes			109c
The Body and Blood of Christ			109d

SACRAMENTS OF HEALING

RECONCILIATION

Forgive us our trespasses	Luke 11:4	Calligraphy	111a
Reconciliation symbol			111b
The right hand of the Lord . . .	Psalm 118:16-17		111c

ANOINTING OF THE SICK

Symbol of anointing			113a
All things whatever you ask in prayer	Mark 11:24	Calligraphy	113b
He has done all things well	Mark 7:37	Calligraphy	113c

SACRAMENTS OF VOCATION

MARRIAGE

Rejoice with those who rejoice	Rom 12:15-16	Calligraphy	115a
Marriage symbol			115b
Cross with rings			115c
Cana wedding scene	John 2:1-11		115d

HOLY ORDERS

Ordination symbols			117a
Go out to the whole world	Mark 16:15	Calligraphy	117b
As priest, Jesus offered his life . . .		Calligraphy	117c